The Batsford Colour Book of The Cotswolds

THE BATSFORD COLOUR BOOK OF
The Cotswolds

Introduction and Commentaries by
Garry Hogg

HASTINGS HOUSE NEW YORK

Acknowledgments

The Publishers wish to thank the following for permission to reproduce the photographs appearing in this book:

J. Allan Cash for page 47
Noel Habgood for pages 19, 21, 31, 57 and 59
A. F. Kersting for pages 17, 23, 29, 33–37, 43, 45 and 51
Kenneth Scowen for pages 25, 27, 39, 41, 49, 53, 55, 61 and 63.

First published 1973

© B. T. Batsford Ltd 1973

Filmset by Servis Filmsetting Ltd, Manchester
Printed and bound in Great Britain by
Wm. Clowes & Sons Ltd, Beccles, Suffolk
for the publishers B. T. Batsford Ltd
4 Fitzhardinge Street, London W1H 0AH

ISBN 0 7134 0024 2

Contents

Introduction

When parcelling up the distinctive regions of Britain, we refer to the English Lakes, the Yorkshire Dales, the Norfolk Broads, the Welsh Marches, the Sussex Downs, and so forth; but it may be said with confidence that no single area is more homogeneous, more integrated, more compact than that region-beyond-compare that answers to and indeed amply fulfils its compact name: the Cotswolds.

What accounts for this homogeneity, this immediately and unquestionably recognisable character that distinguishes it from the other characterful regions vying with it for our appreciation, admiration, and indeed love? Why, quite simply the uniform and pervasive relationship between the oolitic limestone that lies so close beneath the surface of the sparse turf and the buildings large and small, dignified and humble – the churches and manor houses, the tithe barns and cart sheds and drystone walls – that have been fashioned by generations of gifted but anonymous craftsmen transmuting the raw material that lay beneath their feet into products whose sheer beauty of texture and hue as well as design persistently haunt the memory.

In the Cotswolds the buildings more truly seem to have grown out of the soil in which their footings were laid than anywhere else in Britain. You may point to the rival claims of Cornish granite; of Devonshire thatch-and-cob; of half-timbering in Suffolk, Cheshire and Herefordshire; of the slate of North Wales and Cumberland and Westmorland. But he is partisan indeed who would seriously attempt to substantiate such claims. No: Cotswold stone – to the geologist upper and middle lias, inferior oolite and great oolite – possesses a quality to be found nowhere else in quite such various profusion, in quite such widespread perfection.

The oolitic limestone belt may stretch, as the geologists tell us, from the Dorset coast right across the Midlands and well into north Lincolnshire and on into the East Riding of Yorkshire; but it is to be seen at its incomparable best in a quadrilateral no more than 25 miles from north to south and 20 miles from west to east: a bare 500 square miles in all – less by 200 square miles than, for instance, the English Lakes, and infinitely more accessible. Less dramatic, less spectacular, it is true; but with an intimacy of beauty that clutches at the heart, exalts the spirit, pervades one's very being.

Man lived here 4,000 years ago: you will find his most notable burial place, though one only of many, high on Cleeve Cloud on the far western extremity of the Cotswolds, at Belas Knap. Twenty miles to the south, and 20 centuries later, the Romans established a base which they named Corinium and which we know today as Cirencester; it was for long regarded by them as second in importance only to their Londinium. Midway between the ancient burial chamber on Cleeve Cloud and the flourishing city of Corinium lies Chedworth, where you may see today as perfect an example of the civilised Roman's way of life as may be found anywhere in Britain.

Man farmed in the Cotswolds for centuries, and he farms there still. In the Middle Ages there was sheep-rearing here that compared well with that in Suffolk. It is not only Suffolk that possesses superb 'wool' churches such as those at Lavenham and Kersey and Blythburgh; the Cotswolds can match them – at Cirencester, for example, and at Burford, at Fairford and North-leach, and at the two 'Chippings', the market towns of Campden and Norton. Here are churches either originally built or subsequently enlarged and elaborately beautified by wool merchants who had made fortunes in their trade and, like their counterparts in East Anglia, took pleasure as well as pride in building to the glory of their God. Large and small, Cirencester or Coln St Dennis, they are of Cotswold stone that has flowered from beneath the soil into edifices gracious, strong, memorable and true. The wool merchants have been dead and gone these many years; the inscriptions on their tombs have been worn away by time; but the evidence of their piety survives. How many sheep grazed on these wolds – these 'rolling uplands' as they are usually defined – in their heyday no man has authoritatively placed on record; but though it is accepted that the sheep population has now declined, flocks totalling at least 100,000 still peacefully graze the acres on which their forbears throve in times gone by.

So far, no attempt has been made to delineate this unique region; it is time that this should be done, even though purists may challenge what is about to be set down. For those who know – and therefore love – the Cotswolds are strongly partisan. They demand that such-and-such a village be included, and that such-and-such another be excluded. The hamlets of Great and Little Tew, for instance, seem to be a permanent bone of contention: too near to Oxford, some declare; too remote from the 'real' Cotswolds. A fig for such utterances! True, the stone of that lovely pair of villages has something of the darkness of hue that is found more consistently in Northamptonshire, where the oolite has been infiltrated by iron. But is not the style of building (as well as its basic raw material) as truly Cotswold as that to be found in, let us say, Lower Swell, or Adlestrop – particularly, perhaps, Adlestrop, of which Edward Thomas wrote and where also the stone has this rich hue even though the hamlet is within a mile or two of the true heart of the Cotswolds, Stow-on-the-Wold? In support of their objection, some will point out that many of the buildings in Great and Little Tew are roofed with thatch rather than with the traditional Cotswold tiles.

Let us, then, boldly state our own view. Our irregular quadrilateral shall have as its top-left (or north-west) corner a point close to Evesham, in Worcestershire. A line drawn on the map southwards from that point will safely include Broadway, still in that county, a township regarded by many as the most perfect expression of the man-made Cotswold scene. There are, however, those who will say that it errs on the side of 'band-box' perfection and should really yield pride of place to Naunton or Bibury or, even more emphatically, Chipping Campden. Comfortably within that western boundary line will be found Stanton and Stanway, Laverton, Temple Guiting and Guiting Power, Kineton, Chedworth, Ampney Crucis, Coln St Dennis and Coln St Aldwyns, Ampney St Mary and Ampney St Peter. And so to Cirencester itself, whose church, with that of Northleach, is the most splendid example of the flowering of a noble 'wool' church in the whole of the Cotswolds.

From Cirencester the southern boundary of this region may be said to follow pretty closely the line of the Thames itself, whose headwaters are to be found close to this town, just to the south-west of it at Thames Head (though there are some who, despite the ruling of the Thames Authority, still maintain that the river has its true source not far away at the melodiously and evocatively named 'Seven Springs').

This takes us through Lechlade and Kelmscott (sacred to the memory of of William Morris, whose loyalty to the Cotswolds was absolute. It was he who stoutly declared that Bibury was without peer among the villages that populate the shallow valleys and the wolds he loved so well). We come to a halt at a point just beyond this, where the Windrush flows southwards into the Thames, its Cotswold journey at an end; the point is just to the south of Witney, in Oxfordshire.

With Witney as the south-eastern corner, we take a line northwards that just includes Stonesfield (where some of the finest roofing tiles in all England are quarried, and have been quarried for centuries), Charlbury and Spelsbury, Enstone (with its immeasurably ancient 'Hoar Stone', one more reminder that prehistoric man once lived here) and, of course, Chipping Norton. Thence, still northwards, on a line that just enables us to include Great and Little Tew (whatever misguided purists may maintain to the contrary!); it is sufficient for me that H. J. Massingham himself included them in his ever-memorable *Cotswold Country*. This eastern boundary-line ends not far from one of the most beautiful, and beautifully sited, of all England's Stately Homes, bearing the euphonious name of Compton Wynyates. The temptation is to continue northwards just a little farther, if only to include that loveliest of villages on the Oxfordshire–Warwickshire border, Wroxton; but the temptation must somehow be resisted, though the village has almost as good a claim to inclusion as Great and Little Tew. Some justification for its exclusion lies in the fact that if one goes too far north along this line one finds that Warwickshire is making a bold southwards thrust into the true Cotswolds; this breaks the rule that, with the rarest of exceptions (Broadway, in Worcestershire, for instance) the Cotswolds are shared between Gloucestershire, to the west, and Oxfordshire to the east; let no other county seek to disrupt this homogeneity!

The general contour of the region may be said to fall gradually from west to east. The great escarpment that runs north-eastwards from Cheltenham, with its apotheosis at Cleeve Cloud which prehistoric man selected as the site for the finest Long Barrow he ever constructed, Belas Knap, comfortably tops the 1,000-foot mark. Eastwards from here the landscape flows and swells, revives and dies away, seeking lower contours all the time, though occasionally heaving itself upwards for a mile or two as though determined to regain once more the splendour of Cleeve Cloud before succumbing to the lowlands of Oxfordshire and the Thames Valley beyond. Now and then it seems about to achieve this objective. The wolds rise to 600, to 700, to 800 and even 900 feet; but these heights are exceptional. With every few eastward miles covered, the average height above sea level has perceptibly dropped, and before long an altitude of 500 feet is rare and the contour lines on your one-inch map bear modest numbers such as 400, 300, and even less. No matter: England in general slopes downwards from west to east; with the exception of the Wye and the Mersey our greatest rivers flow eastwards into the North Sea. In remote times even the Thames was no more than a tributary of the Rhine.

What, then, is the general character of the Cotswolds? It is not difficult to describe in bare terms: rolling uplands (highlands is too grandiose a term) interspersed with shallow meandering valleys in which modest streams wind leisurely. The word 'lazy' has been used of these, and it is apt enough, save for the fact that the connotation of the word is less happy than that of the word 'leisurely'. It may have been first applied to these streams by wool men who had been exasperated by the fact that nowhere could they find, or engineer, a 'fall' of water powerful enough to operate mill-wheels that would drive the machinery required to process their products. Such mills did exist; more were planned; but to lead water to them in quantity sufficient to provide the requisite power was rarely a viable or economic proposition, so there was a tendency for such factories – rural indeed by today's standards – to be moved westwards to where there was a more reliable and constant supply of fast-moving water.

The Cotswolds, as has been indicated, are essentially divided between the two counties, Gloucestershire and Oxfordshire. The border between them runs unevenly from south to north, with the larger portion of the region lying to the west of it. Stow-on-the-Wold could be taken as the central point of the 500 square miles area. Through the centre of this town runs the rule-straight Fosse Way, a road laid out by the Romans in a straight line from south-west to north-east across the county from Corinium (Cirencester) to Lindum Colonia (Lincoln). The individual towns and villages are neatly distributed on either side of it, to west and to east. That rare quartet of hamlets, Upper and Lower Swell, Upper and Lower Slaughter, lie to the west of it; they are matched, a little to the south, by Coln St Dennis, Coln Rogers and Coln St Aldwyns, a trio that take their name from the stream called the Coln that flows down the valley that enfolds them. Another little trio, also taking their names from the stream that links them, will be found not far away: Ampney St Mary, Ampney St Peter and Ampney Crucis; if its near neighbour, the sombrely named Down Ampney, may be included, then the trio becomes a quartet.

One of the minor charms of the Cotswolds is to be found in its galaxy of names: names euphonious, names evocative and suggestive, names that linger in the memory even though, in rare cases, the place they stand for is not particularly memorable. Where in all England, for instance, will you find a stream with a more charming name than Windrush? Where, for that matter, even in the Cotswolds, will you encounter a more mellifluously named stream than Evenlode? Every other hamlet that you come to as you wander along these valleys or breast one wold to descend leisurely into the next one seems to offer a more alluring invitation to explore. You may already have admired the great 'wool' church of Northleach, just off the Fosse Way and marking the headwaters of the Leach. Follow the stream southwards to its junction with the Thames near Kelmscott, and you will pass through Eastleach Turville and Eastleach Martin – both faithful to the stream that links them. Near the latter there is a fine example of that most ancient type of bridge, the clapper.

There is, so to speak, a twinship between stream and hamlet to be met with all over the Cotswolds. The village of Evenlode shares its name with the stream that flows by it, as do the hamlets scattered like small jewels along the bright threads of Ampney, Coln and Leach. Other places have names no less beautiful, even though they do not share them with a named stream. Shipton-under-Wychwood is one such, with its near neighbours, Ascott-under-Wychwood and Milton-under-Wychwood. Here the shared part-name is that of a great forest that once spread over this whole region to the north of Burford. Like so many forests in medieval times, this was a royal hunting preserve. One does not think of the Cotswolds, today, as forest land, though there are magnificent stands of beeches; but the very word 'wold' is cognate with 'weald', and the Teutonic *wald* – all referring to afforested territory. The *Shaven Crown* at Shipton-under-Wychwood, six centuries old, was once a royal hunting lodge; but much earlier than that it was the guest hospice for the important Abbey of Bruern. The name it bears is a tacit reminder of its monastic origin, and the tonsure of course appears on its sign.

There is indeed no limit to the evocative quality, to the sheer melodiousness, of the names of villages and minuscule hamlets that are to be found sequestered in the valleys and on the slopes of these wolds. Winson and Quenington are two examples – each incidentally with a small church that amply repays a visit. Temple Guiting and Guiting Power, twelve miles to the north, on the Windrush, strike perhaps an alien note, but you will find there no less true an example of the essential Cotswold scene and, close to the latter village, one of the most beautiful and beautifully sited of the smaller manor houses anywhere to be found.

A pair of small townships, or larger villages, share the name Bourton; one of these is 'on-the-Hill', the other is 'on-the-Water'. The stream flows beneath a series of charming little bridges – virtually miniatures – that constitute perhaps the outstanding feature of this Bourton. Like Broadway, some 12 miles to the north-west, this Bourton is perhaps a little too self-aware, too anxious to remind the visitor that here is something rather special. Well, 'rather special' it must be agreed that it is, and it should not be condemned out of hand on that account, for it displays its wares generously and people come eagerly enough to sample them; why should they not, anyway?

Few roads of any size span this quadrilateral 20 miles by 25; so much the better! It is the smaller roads, the lanes, that prove so rewarding. It is these that will lead you to the treasures you might otherwise miss. The charming Museum of Bygones at Evenlode, for example, lovingly assembled over the years and cleverly displayed by one dedicated woman in her home, the Old School House. Another, of a somewhat different type, is tucked away in the hamlet of Filkins – a name which might have come out of the pages of Dickens. Farther to the south still, indeed on the very edge of the Cotswolds, the home of William Morris, artist and craftsman, at Kelmscott.

But you may explore these minor roads, these winding lanes, without any specific objective, and always be amply rewarded. For, as was said at the outset, there is an impression of compactness here: a tacit suggestion that at every turn, whether advertised or not, there will be something to reward you. And always there is this essential element of stone. There is stone just beneath your feet; stone flowers into the simple beauty of cottage and cart shed, of soaring church tower, of manor house and farm. Your road may be bounded by drystone walls, and drystone walls will run across the wolds into the distance, intersected here and there by boundary walls between field and field. As among the Pennines (though this stone is mellow, creamy-white, golden, tawny, and often incandescent in the glow of evening sunshine) these walls are a dominant feature of the landscape; they knit it together, accentuate its curves and contours, give it perspective as well as contributing to its character.

Nowhere, surely, in all Britain has the stone of a region been more perfectly, memorably utilised and worked? It is a mistake to think that the term 'architecture' can be rightly used only of splendid examples of great or classic building. Certainly it would be a gross mistake here in the Cotswolds. For it does not need a professional eye to note that virtually every building, large and small, from church and manor house to the humblest stile, bears the imprint of the man who designed and constructed it. The architect may be as anonymous as the stonemason who executed his orders, but his signature is there. This undeniable fact partly accounts for the degree of homogeneity that characterises this compact area.

Note, for example, the steep pitch of all the roofs. This is not in anticipation of heavy falls of snow and the need to shed it without delay; it is because all buildings (save for a lamentable few that have been re-roofed with slate or some man-made material) are roofed with stone slabs, generally referred to as tiles but sometimes as 'slates' even though one thinks of these as emanating from Welsh quarries. These slabs, even when they have been thinly split, are enormously heavy, comparable with the Horsham slabs in Sussex; however stoutly hewn, the oak roof timbers would be hard put to it to support the dead-weight of such slabs if the roof were of normal pitch. While noting these roofs, your eye may be held by a traditional feature that is most subtly pleasing: the tiles are graded so that the smallest run along immediately beneath the ridge; thereafter, the tiles are increased in size outwards and downwards so that the largest of them form the eaves. The judgment called for here and exercised so skilfully is but one of the traditional skills that the Cotswold stonemason and tiler have always possessed.

The steep pitch of these roofs, however, is relieved by the infinite variety of gable and dormer window inset among them. While the dominating lines of any house will be its horizontals – primarily at eave level and ridge – there are the shorter verticals to emphasise these basic lines; and, as a bonus, so to speak, the trimly proportioned angles that form the gable ends, and the little dormers, so often set not at eave level but part way up, or down, the steep front pitch of the roof. And there are the satisfying smaller details, too: the moulded drip-stones over the upper windows; the ratio of mullion to transom in the larger windows of the manor houses but also in the diminutive windows of the humblest cottage; the relation of window-space to façade generally, whether on large scale or small. The spacing and poise of the chimneys, too, indicate the artist-cum-craftsman at work rather than simply a stonemason religiously carrying out instructions laid down by an employer.

There is limitless variety among details such as these as well as in the major aspects of the landscape as a whole. It is a variety too great to be accommodated in what can, after all, be nothing more than one Cotswold lover's heartfelt recommendation of a region he has always placed in a class by itself to others who may know it already and love it as he does; and to those – the more fortunate, perhaps – who have yet to explore it for the first time and so make it their own.

Stow-on-the-Wold

At 800 feet, this is the highest township in the Cotswolds. Incidentally, it is one of the very few place-names that specifically identify their own location. In its heyday it was the setting for the most flourishing wool market in all England, and there are records of no fewer than 20,000 sheep being bought and sold there on one market day alone. It is hardly surprising, therefore, that its market place, with its traditional market cross, is so large.

Stow may be said to represent the geographical centre of the region, and it is to be noted that as many as eight important roads (including the Roman-built Fosse Way) pass through it, radiating from its centre like the spokes of a wheel. The great market place is surrounded by houses built of a stone that is perhaps somewhat greyer than that to be seen in the 'show' villages such as Broadway. This tacitly suggests that Stow has always been a place of business rather than of retired leisure, though by the standards of today's industrial centres this, of course, is nonsense. Nevertheless, there is a sense of purposefulness and occupation here; as there always has been. The old posting-house, *The King's Arms,* shown in the photograph, was used more than four centuries ago as a lodging for the couriers of King Edward VI.

Lower Slaughter

Like Broadway, though on a very much smaller scale, this village is something of a show-piece. Its one narrow, curving street runs parallel with the sparkling stream, a minor tributary of the Windrush. A mill wheel turns slowly at the entrance to the village; the cottages stand back from the water behind sloping turf banks, approached by miniature footbridges with white rails and shaded here and there by beeches and limes. At the far end is the green, with a shop or two, facing the manor house which stands back somewhat reservedly behind a screen of trees with the stream flowing past at their feet.

Traffic does not, indeed cannot, flow along this very minor road, as it can through Broadway, Campden and the Bourtons. Thus the village is perpetually a place of almost complete silence: just the ripple of water, the plash of the mill wheel on the days when it is turning, the call of a mother from a small window to her child playing on the nearest bridge, the rustle of the breeze in the foliage screening the tiled roofs. Those who know the charmed Dutch village of Giethoorn will find something of the same rural magic here.

Upper Slaughter

Though one of a named pair, this is generally less well regarded by the sightseer than Lower Slaughter. It may be because its charms are more subtle, not so immediately obvious; but they are nevertheless well worth looking for and, eventually, as rewarding. It is built on a slope, and the best approach is from below rather than from above. The climbing road, enclosed by walls, brings you to a tiny triangle, with the church half-screened by stone cottages and approached through its graveyard by a path sunk deep below turf level.

Inside the church is a plaque expressing the gratitude of the small community that, though it sent its menfolk to fight in two world wars, did not lose a single life. This is a village very much alive and at work today: a busy farm lies almost in its heart and men come and go, oblivious of the sightseer who lingers beneath the great chestnut tree outside the church gate, having fallen victim to its insidious charms. At the top of the rise, behind and above the village is one of the finest Elizabethan manor houses anywhere in the Cotswolds.

Burford

Like Bourton and Broadway, this lovely little town (it has outgrown village status) has a wide main street. This not only dips steeply from the almshouses at the top to the ancient church on the banks of the Windrush at its feet, but is also tilted sideways so that one row of variegated buildings lining it stands higher than those facing it across the stretches of turf and pollarded limes that separate them from the roadway.

It is said that in Burford you can see examples of every variety of style in Cotswold building, and anything more than a perfunctory glance will prove the truth of the statement. The stonework, as always, is exquisite, and present in every hue from palish grey to rich umber. But here in Burford – thanks to the relative proximity of the former forest of Wychwood – there is half-timbering too. This is not, of course, characteristic of the Cotswolds, but it nevertheless blends with the traditional most harmoniously (as in this photograph of Sheep Street). There are buildings here of every date from the thirteenth century upwards; not the least interesting of them is the fifteenth-century Tolsey, or Market Hall, where, as the name implies, tolls were once exacted.

Minster Lovell

One of the most mellifluously named of the villages on the Windrush.
There is hardly a hint of any monastic tradition today and only the last
ruins of the 'moated grange' long occupied by the ill-fated Lovells, the
reputed setting for the traditional 'Mistletoe Bough' legend. Here,
allegedly, the skeletons of Francis Lovell and his faithful hound were
discovered sealed up in a small room in 1718, two and a half centuries
after they died there of starvation.

The ruins are overlooked by a cluster of stone-built cottages, many of
them thatched, though the attractive *Swan Inn*, for which the village is
perhaps best known today, is roofed with the finest of all Cotswold slates,
those from the famous Stonesfield quarry. The church was built in the
mid-fifteenth century by one of the Lovells; much of it has been not too
successfully restored, but it still contains some of its fifteenth-century glass,
among its proudest possessions. Because it lies well off any highway, and
is approached by an old bridge, it may be hoped that Minster Lovell will
remain untouched, unspoiled, and live down the haunting tales with
which its eventful past has for so long been associated.

Bourton-on-the-Water

'It is the little Windrush – that friend of villages – which makes the loveliness of Bourton': so wrote a Cotswolds lover 40 years ago. Here that stream has widened to some 30 feet and become so shallow that its waters flow like a moving mirror only inches deep over a weed-strewn, golden gravel bed. They run parallel with the main street from the weir and mill at one end to the *New Inn* (by no means new, in fact) at the other, behind which is a scale-model of the little township, the delight of children young and old.

A sense of lightness and brightness permeates Bourton, due in part to the prevalence of running water, and in part to the cleanliness of the stone of which the houses overlooking it, many of them up to four centuries old, are built. Any shadows to be found lie beneath the scattered trees on the roadside lawns and beneath the succession of low-arched ornamental bridges linking them. Do not be put off by the *cliché* that Bourton-on-the-Water is the 'Venice of Britain'; it is not. It is a Cotswold township that exists in its own unquestioned right.

Kelmscott

On the south-easternmost fringe of the Cotswolds, this is the sequestered
'Nowhere' of William Morris's *News from Nowhere*; probably almost all
who go in search of this place do so, not so much for beautiful stonework
(which indeed is to be found in generous measure) as in the guise of
pilgrims to the shrine of this artist-craftsman's home. Morris, founder
with Burne-Jones of the pre-Raphaelite Movement, bought the
Elizabethan manor house here just over a century ago and with his wife
and Burne-Jones and others, formed a compact local unit, of which for a
time Rossetti was a member.

When he died, just a quarter of a century later, he was buried in the
graveyard of the twelfth-century church. Kelmscott, which he so dearly
loved and cherished, gave its name to the printing-press on which this
social reformer produced so many of his manifestoes, though it was in fact
situated in Hammersmith rather than in this stone country. But it was
from the Cotswolds that much of his inspiration derived; and it was he
who dubbed Bibury, not many miles away, the most beautiful village in
the whole of the region in which he had made his home.

Bibury

Of this enchanting village you might well comment: '*Multum in Parvo*', for it is unusually well endowed. The Coln flows through it; at one end an old coaching inn overlooks a trout hatchery and, beyond this, a massively buttressed mill house reached by way of a fine eighteenth-century bridge. Follow the rippling Coln downstream and you pass in front of slanting Rack Field, so called because here wool was dried after it had come from the 'factory' that occupied part of these low-slung, heavily dormered early-seventeenth-century linked cottages, Arlington Row, now happily preserved by the National Trust.

Not far away is the thirteenth-century church, which incorporates some Anglo-Saxon work; you must pass through one of the rare 'squeeze-belly' stiles to enter the churchyard, overlooked by the village school. Across the green is a noble stand of beeches, the native Cotswold tree. Their pale green contrasts sweetly with the stone of the variously placed buildings large and small. A hundred years ago, William Morris – artist–craftsman–sociologist – declared Bibury to be the most beautiful village in the whole region; he would be a bold man who challenged so authoritative a judgment.

Fairford

This township is situated on the southern fringe of the Cotswolds, and some people may consider that it lacks the true Cotswold 'feel'. Because it lies on a busy road it is perhaps best seen first from the near side of a stream overlooked by a gabled mill house. From this view point, the sky-line is dominated by the tower of one of the finest of all the 'wool' churches, soaring upwards from the trees outspread at its feet.

Though it is of later date than many Cotswold churches larger and smaller, it possesses a unique display of magnificent stained glass, no fewer than 28 windows in all and so among the most numerous of their kind in all England. Between them they tell the Bible story, from the Creation to the Crucifixion, from the Acts of the Apostles to the Last Judgment. The final picture in this glorious sequence is quite horrifying in its detail. Local tradition, loath as always to die, holds that this glass was salvaged from a wrecked ship; authority, however, states that it was designed specifically for the church when the original fabric was restored by a merchant who had made a fortune in wool.

Coln St Aldwyns

One of the trio that derive their name from the stream that links them, the stripling Coln. Which of them, in the fairy-tale phrase, is 'the fairest of the three'? The choice is not easy. All have water running close beside them; all are of true Cotswold stone, hewn and assembled in the traditional Cotswold manner; there is little to choose among them for size. Because the ground slopes, the cottages tend to stray towards the water, as though unable to resist its allure. But then, why should they resist?

Here a mill still stands at the foot of the village, once a vital amenity, now but a quiet reminder of the past. The broad leaves of chestnut trees offer shade immediately outside the small post office, and the public telephone is to be found, not in a red-painted kiosk but in its own little house of local stone, constructed with as much care as any of the other and larger buildings. You enter the post office beneath a steep-gabled porch that has the classic proportions of all those thousands of gables large and small that give character to Cotswold buildings the length and breadth of the region.

Cirencester

With justifiable pride this town calls itself the Capital of the Cotswolds; no one, surely, would challenge the claim. Fifteen centuries ago, standing as it does at the junction of a network of major Roman roads, including the Fosse Way, it was the capital city of its province. In medieval days it was the chief wool market for the huge sheep-rearing area on whose western borders it stands. Small wonder, then, that its church of St John the Baptist is one of the glories not merely of the region but of all England.

Its superb tower soars above one of the most beautiful porches in the country. This Gothic edifice rises to three storeys, its great bay windows topped by a battlemented parapet. The carving, both within and without, is so beautiful that it catches the breath as it holds the eye. It dominates the open market place, which has witnessed exchange and mart for centuries; because it was long used for judicial and other secular purposes it was known for many years as the Town Hall. The Roman province comes to life here, in their ancient Corinium; and not far from the church is the Corinium Museum which gives a clear and impressive picture of life here as it was 19 centuries ago.

Eastleach Martin

Like Eastleach Turville, its neighbour a stone's throw distant, this hamlet takes its name from the stream they share with Northleach, a larger township altogether. At the entrance to the hamlet the stream is spanned by the type of bridge familiar to those who know Postbridge and Dartmeet: the so-called clapper. It looks immensely ancient, for the clapper is the earliest stone bridge known to us; in fact it is little more than a century old, but its style is absolutely right for a shallow stream threading water-meadows.

You could well find yourself virtually alone when you enter the hamlet, for it is not on any through-road and is anyway somewhat overshadowed by its larger neighbour. But it is worth a leisurely visit, if only for the simple little church, its focal point. Small (as befits so small a community), this is of Norman origin, notably the exquisite little porch, with Early English features that marry perfectly with the rest to make an integrated whole, dominated by a squat, square tower nicely proportioned to the modest edifice it adorns.

Westwell

This hamlet is less familiar to lovers of the Cotswold scene than places with well-known names like the Bourtons, the Slaughters and Chipping Campden. Yet it is to be found neatly placed between the Cirencester and the Lechlade roads leading to Burford, and only three miles from that admirable centre for exploration. This is not only a characteristically Cotswold but a typically English village, for here is the traditional village green, its focal point, together with an almost perfectly circular village pond, overlooked on one side by a bank of trees and on the other by the mullioned windows and gable-ends of the manor house.

Closer to the pond there is the plinth carrying the squared shaft of an old cross, its steps worn smooth by generations of villagers who have sat on them, contemplating the quiet water and its occupants. Behind the trees, yet close enough to be part of the grouped houses and cottages, is the church, standing on a small hill so that its belfry keeps a watchful eye on events, as it has done down the centuries. Not the least noticeable feature of Westwell is the series of curving drystone walls enclosing farmyards and stands of trees and knitting the whole hamlet together.

Cotswold Farmstead

Unlike such dairy-farming and cattle-breeding districts as, for instance, neighbouring Herefordshire, Cotswold farmsteads in general are relatively small as well as compact. No need for cow-byres and rick-yards here; the flocks, whether their numbers run into thousands or only into hundreds or less, are out on the wolds the year round, grazing the thin turf between the miles of undulating drystone walls that are a characteristic feature of the landscape.

But these farmsteads, of whatever size, were, like the 'wool' churches and manor houses, the town halls, posting inns, cottages, bridges and virtually every man-made structure, built of the local stone. Within only a few yards of them, very often, saucer-shaped depressions in the ground indicate where the quarry was from which the stone that went to their building was extracted; to build from stone on-site was an economy sensibly practised by Cotswold men right from the beginning.

In this picture, the stone-slab roofs are now so thickly encrusted with lichen that they have almost the sombre tones of weathered tiles. Nevertheless, all that is depicted, whether house, outbuilding or containing wall, is, as always, of the oolitic limestone that lies so close beneath the turf: a unifying factor that affords instant aesthetic pleasure.

Northleach

This small town stands just clear of the busy Fosse Way and close to the source of the Leach, which gives its name also to Eastleach Martin and Eastleach Turville many zigzagging miles south-eastwards en route for the Thames. Like Stow-on-the-Wold, it was an immensely prosperous wool town, and its chief glory is the magnificent fifteenth-century 'wool' church, in Perpendicular style, with a particularly fine South Porch, buttressed and pinnacled and perfectly proportioned to the great church to which it gives access.

Detail here, not always immediately apparent, is well worth looking for. An example is the fine brass commemorating one John Fortey, a patron of the church who, like so many, made his money out of sheep; appropriately enough, he is depicted there with his feet resting on a woolsack. A smaller, no less memorable, detail is a grotesque, the work of some medieval stone-mason with (as so often) a sense of humour. The carving is of a cat playing the fiddle to – of all unlikely audiences – a trio of rats! But though undoubtedly the finest, the church is only one of many true Cotswold buildings large and small set about the sloping market place; and such new ones as have been built have been designed with care so as to harmonise with those that precede them by so many centuries.

Cotswold Viewpoint

These rolling uplands and intersecting valleys are beautiful in themselves, possessing an individual quality that cannot be paralleled anywhere else in England. Here trees – mainly beech – grow in isolated stands rather than in serried masses; thus it is everywhere possible to obtain wide-ranging views from the higher contours.

Nowhere are these to be obtained more satisfyingly, indeed on a grander scale, than on the western fringe. For here, as has been shown, the ground is generally higher, rising impressively towards the great west escarpment that runs north-eastwards from Cheltenham. It is no exaggeration to state that one of the half-dozen most satisfying long-distance views in southern England is to be obtained from this escarpment.

It offers a magnificent prospect across low-lying terrain north-westwards to the Malvern Hills and south-westwards to the Forest of Dean, on the far side of the Severn Valley, and beyond that, across the serpentining Wye Valley well into Herefordshire and, on a clear day at any rate, to the beautiful if inappropriately named Black Mountains and Brecon Beacons across the Welsh Border. Lush pasturage and valley slopes tree-filled and sunlit are framed within an undulating horizon of infinite allure.

46

Painswick

This memorable village lies so far to the west that it barely qualifies for inclusion as 'Cotswold'. Yet there is no doubting the provenance of the stone of which its houses and church are built: this is Cotswold all right! Though it lies on a main road, here this is narrow and tortuous. But it is well worth finding somewhere to leave the car and make for what is undoubtedly Painswick's most famous feature: the assembly of just 99 magnificent yew trees, planted almost exactly 200 years ago and maintained in impeccable condition by expert clippers in the churchyard. It is believed locally that no 'hundredth yew tree' would ever take root.

Look up from among them, and you will see an early-seventeenth-century needle spire tapering into the sky above the tower of the fifteenth-century church. You might be fortunate enough to find yourself here on the Sunday nearest to 19 September, when the traditional annual 'clipping' takes place. This, however, does not refer to the trimming of the yews but to a ceremony of much more ancient significance and one of the most charmingly picturesque still to be found in England where, happily, traditions die hard.

Stanton

A Cotswold village of quite exceptional modest charm. Its single, narrow street climbs gently from the sixteenth-century Stanton House to the *Mount Inn* on the crest of the hill, from which a superb panorama reaches to the Bredon and Malvern Hills. The two rows of buildings crowd close to it on either side, so much so that you almost trip over their doorsteps. Each is a little gem in honey-hued stone that turns to old-gold as the sun lowers towards the west, and the old-gold to the deeper tones of ochre as the minutes pass.

Massingham said that Stanton is 'more intimately Cotswold, a village more authentic than Stanway', its near neighbour, and reminds us (as if the discerning were in need of this!) that many of its small houses belong to what he calls 'the best period of Cotswold architecture, from 1570 to 1650'. You can verify this by date for yourself, for one cottage is clearly marked '1577' and another not far from it, '1618'. The connoisseurs, who may find Broadway, for example, too immaculate for their liking, will certainly not find this less-assuming Cotswold village disappointing in any respect.

Stanway

Like the Swells and the Slaughters, this is one of a pair of neighbouring villages (the other is Stanton); though both are true Cotswold, they could hardly be more unlike. In former times – surprisingly for its size – this was a busy little place: a corn mill, a cider mill, a fulling-mill, and even a paper mill. Not so today, however. Though, as always in this region, its cottages have charm, Stanway's chief claim to distinction lies in a group of fine buildings consisting of a giant tithe-barn, once attached to the Abbey of Tewkesbury and built six centuries ago; a church whose date also is the fourteenth century; and a manor house of the early sixteenth century (youthful by comparison).

Its dominant feature is this splendid gate-house in Renaissance style, attributed with confidence to no less a figure than Inigo Jones. Church, tithe-barn and manor house stand side by side, closely related though of different centuries. They are Stanway's pride, and their grouping is as traditional as is that of the humbler dwellings that constitute the remainder of this little village.

Snowshill

This village clings to a steepish fold in one of the lesser escarpments that break the general wolds contours, and at first impact gives the impression of not being wholly integrated. This is partly because the buildings have had to be spaced about wherever there was room for them on one or other of the interlaced slopes. There is no 'main street', as such, and the houses – almost every one of them individually beautiful – are set at odd angles to one another.

Another reason lies in the fact that the church, usually the focal point of any village, is little more than 100 years old and built in a pseudo-Gothic style that can never blend with the other, traditionally-styled buildings. But compensation lies in the beauty and age of the sixteenth-century manor house, now National Trust property. It dominates this endearingly straggling congeries of houses, every one of which is tilted one way or the other athwart the horizon. The most rewarding view of the village is a roof-top one from the narrow road that skirts Snowshill ('Sno'zl' to the initiate) on its upper edge, climbing as it were reluctantly away from it.

Broadway

Let us face it: this is a 'show piece' – the Cotswold village *par excellence*.
Its seventeenth-century hotel is famous; the buildings lining the wide
main street (aptly justifying the name) are all of mellow Cotswold stone,
each immaculately maintained though many date back 400 years; the
gardens that front the street as you climb towards Fish Hill give the
impression of vying with one another to attract the eye – as indeed may
well be the case, for Broadway has long claimed to be 'the most
beautiful village in England', a claim not easy to challenge.

There is inspiration in its layout. Look at it in detail. The rows of
cottages have each their bow window, their dormers breaking the line
of the roof that links them one to the other; now and then an unexpected
gable-end protrudes, and an upper storey carries a heightened roof inset
with dormers and surmounted by chimney-stacks set perhaps at right-
angles to the others. The slates are beautifully graduated, showing to
perfection this genius of the slater's craft. The greensward spreads like an
apron at the cottages' feet, impeccably trimmed, velvety smooth.

Ebrington

Ask for this hamlet of a local and you may well be met with a stare of incomprehension; for to many it is still known as 'Yabberton'. Like Sussex's Heathfield and Nottinghamshire's Gotham (among scores of other such 'lost' hamlets), it has acquired a mythology of its own, of which its inhabitants are by no means ashamed. Here, the oldsters may still tell you over a pint of half-and-half, the hedges were grown high to prevent the cuckoo from flying away; here, too, manure was spread round the base of the church tower to encourage it to 'grow' at least to the same height as a rival tower – though it may not be admitted by all that the practice still obtains in this eighth decade of the twentieth century.

For all that, Ebrington possesses the popular element of 'the quaint'. It lies, contentedly enough, well off the beaten track; many of the cottages still favour thatch rather than Cotswold slate, for the homeliness and sense of being cherished that this time-honoured roofing material affords them. Narrow lanes dip and rise and dip again, and signposts are low-set, as though for the use of those not yet grown to maturity.

Chipping Campden

To many, this is the first name that springs to mind when the Cotswolds are mentioned; and not surprisingly, for it contains all that is essentially Cotswold in character and tradition. It was one of the great centres of wool trading in the Middle Ages. The men who made fortunes out of wool built there, and built to last, whether it was the superb Market Hall, among the most famous single buildings in all England, or their own private residences which proliferate along the main street.

In their piety, also, men who had made their money in the region, and their descendants who retained a sense of gratitude, built almshouses such as these, dating from the very early years of the seventeenth century, raised above street level on a wide terrace with a capped stone parapet. Beyond these, a little higher up the slope, rises the tower of yet another magnificent 'wool' church, mainly Perpendicular in style but containing evident traces of late-Norman stonework. A dignity, almost an impression of monastic calm, pervades this town, marking it out distinctly from perhaps all other Cotswold towns; here the past is consistently, pervasively present.

Great Tew

This minuscule hamlet lies sequestered, and so all too easily missed, in the bottom of a cup among low hills, tree-embowered, secretive. Its unusually warm-hued stonework peeping in and out of scattered evergreens, its heavy thatch, its pair of stocks on the steeply sloping green that dips to the school house and the homely inn: these suggest age, though in fact Great Tew, like its under-estimated close neighbour, Little Tew, is comparatively modern, having been landscaped by Claudius Loudoun less than 200 years ago.

The church cannot be seen from the village; with the fine manor house, in whose spacious grounds it stands, it will be found part-way up the hill that climbs out of the hollow, approached through an avenue of trees. Parts of it date back to the thirteenth century, and it seems out of proportion to the tiny hamlet it serves. An outstanding characteristic of Great Tew is the depth and weight of its thatch, for once more prevalent than the traditional Cotswold slate. Its depth emphasises the impression gained of wished-for privacy, of a deep desire to remain enclosed, inviolate.